Information Literacy:

A

For ...... Age

THE ASPEN INSTITUTE

Communications and Society Program
Charles M. Firestone
Executive Director
Washington, DC
1999

this report, please contact:

The Aspen Institute
Publications Office
P.O. Box 222
109 Houghton Lab Lane
Queenstown, Maryland 21658
Phone: (410) 820-5326
Fax: (410) 827-9174
E-mail: publications@aspeninstitute.org

For all other inquiries, please contact:

The Aspen Institute
Communications and Society Program
One Dupont Circle, N.W.
Suite 700
Washington, D.C. 20036
Phone: (202) 736-5818
Fax: (202) 467-0790

Charles M. Firestone   Amy Korzick Garmer
Executive Director   *Associate Director*

Contents

Foreword

A healthy democratic society requires a literate citizenry. But what is an *informationally literate* citizenry in the information age? The ability to locate, organize, evaluate, and communicate information takes on new urgency in a world driven increasingly by information and the technologies developed to create, distribute, and manage it. Properly understood, information literacy goes beyond access to the technology itself and addresses barriers to full, effective, and knowledgeable participation in an information society.

The need to address information literacy as an important societal issue is strong and immediate. Individuals and families increasingly need sophisticated information skills and knowledge to take advantage of educational opportunities; to apply for government services or student loans; to manage their health care, finances, and retirement investments; to participate in the political process; and otherwise to make the choices that affect their lives. Those who are least able to navigate the channels of information will continue to fall further behind as information and the knowledge that it yields become the currencies of success in society.

Information literacy is equally important to our economic well-being. Continued growth in markets for communications and information goods and services will hinge on a public that is adept at incorporating information into all aspects of daily life and adopting new skills for using information and technology. Businesses already are experiencing the troubling effects of a workforce with inadequate information and technical skills and are having to invest significant resources in employee training and remediation.

Large segments of the population in the United States today do not have access to an adequate array of information resources. Moreover, such individuals often do not know how to use those resources effectively. This knowledge deficiency extends beyond understanding how to access and use hardware and software resources to learning how to adapt and expand critical thinking and communication skills.

The Aspen Institute Forum on Communications and Society

The Aspen Institute's Forum on Communications and Society (FOCAS) met in Aspen, Colorado, in August 1998 to explore the nature of literacy in the digital age and to consider collaborative strategies that might be undertaken by the public and private sectors to overcome barriers to more widespread information literacy. Specifically, FOCAS participants started to identify the necessary leverage points in society where new learning and partnerships could improve access to information and quality learning opportunities—and ultimately improve the level of information literacy.

FOCAS is a chief executive officer (CEO)-level body that is convened annually by the Aspen Institute to address subjects relating to the societal impact of the communications and information sectors. FOCAS seeks to find ways that communications and information technology can be employed to improve society, first by taking a critical look at how advances in these fields will affect traditional democratic values and institutions and then by asking what policies the private and public sectors should pursue, individually and collectively, to foster a better and more democratic society. In previous years, FOCAS members have addressed the difficult issues of wiring schools and teacher training, lifelong learning, and employability and the changing employment relationship. Because the FOCAS process is geared toward the creation of innovative solutions to societal problems, each meeting has yielded a set of recommendations for collaborative actions that are extremely helpful for understanding the underlying issues and the roles that individuals, corporations, public sector organizations, and governments can play in improving society.

In addressing the issue of information literacy, FOCAS members were guided by a desire to see the benefits of information and new technologies enjoyed more broadly by individuals and throughout society by enhancing:

- skills for basic self-sufficiency;
- participation in economic, political, and social life;
- overall quality of life;
- adaptability to change;
- a sense of achievement and self-fulfillment; and
- the promotion of democratic values (e.g., pluralism).

The Report

This report is an informed observer's interpretation of the discussions that took place at the 1998 annual meeting of FOCAS CEOs in Aspen. (A list of participating FOCAS members appears in the appendix.) Following the summary of deliberations, the report outlines six initiatives suggested by FOCAS members that might be developed further to advance the cause of information literacy. These suggestions are only a few of the many collaborations that are possible. Some are already being tried; others require further development. They are offered here to stimulate further discussion regarding the most workable solutions to the problem of information literacy. The strategies for greater information literacy include the following:

- Take idea leadership to promote awareness of information literacy (including the formation of a national commission to study the impact of information technologies on society).
- Assess and hold educators and political leaders at all levels accountable for students' proficiency in information literacy.
- Give teachers the preparation and support they need to do a better job.
- Involve parents more deeply in their children's education.
- Develop a dramatically different technology-based educational alternative.
- Increase funding for research in education and information literacy.

We should emphasize that this report is one person's interpretation of the conference. We caution the reader that although the record may demonstrate general consensus on some issues, the statements made in this report should not be taken in any way as the views of any particular participant or organization unless otherwise noted. Additionally, although FOCAS members make every attempt to attend the annual meeting, there are times when individual members are unable to do so, and their membership in FOCAS should not be construed as representing their assent to the material in this volume.

As Richard Adler states in his report of the conference, at the beginning of the meeting there was a certain level of discomfort with the phrase *information literacy*, largely because it takes a familiar term—*literacy*—and adds a modifier that is both vague and complex. To make the search for a definition more manageable, participants began by addressing two fundamental questions that underlie the discussion of information literacy: What is the role of information in the lives of individuals, organizations, and institutions? How, if at all, is this relationship changing as new communications and information technologies take hold? Discussion of these questions ultimately yielded the suggestion of a national commission to explore the social significance of the Internet and other new technologies in a civil society.

The discussion then shifted to the barriers that impede the acquisition of the knowledge and skills required to deal effectively with information in its myriad forms, especially digital. The discussion hearkened back to previous FOCAS discussions on learning and technology. In fact, one of the agreements that emerged from the 1997 FOCAS meeting (detailed in the Aspen Institute publication, *Jobs, Technology, and Employability: Redefining the Social Contract*) was that schools "need to do more than simply provide their graduates with specific technical skills. Perhaps the most important skill that students need to prepare themselves for what lies ahead is to 'learn how to learn.'" The pivotal role of the nation's public school system in promoting the skills necessary for information literacy was debated at length. Participants suggested initiatives for working within the formal educational system (e.g., giving teachers the preparation and support they need to do a better job, and holding educators and political leaders at all levels accountable for students' proficiency in information literacy), as well as the more radical idea of creating a dramatically different technology-based educational alternative (the BEST school proposal) that would address the need for information literacy in education.

Acknowledgments

Many people have made significant contributions to the 1998 Forum on Communications and Society. We are especially grateful to FOCAS co-chairs Reed Hundt and Eric Schmidt for contributing their considerable expertise, talent, and insight to the preparation and execution of the 1998 forum meeting. We appreciate the energy and efforts of the participating FOCAS members who convened in Aspen: C. Michael Armstrong, Zoë Baird, James Barr, Asa Briggs, David Britt, Jolynn Barry Butler, John Doerr, Ira Fishman, Stanley Hubbard, Reed Hundt, Michael Jordan, William Kennard, Charles B. Knapp, Michael O. Leavitt, Edward Markey, William Milliken, Peter Price, Rebecca Rimel, Eric Schmidt, Kurt Schmoke, Mark Warner, and Lois Jean White. We also thank Martin Ernst of Harvard University's Program on Information Resources Policy, who served as our resource participant. Other FOCAS members who have been supportive of the project but who were unable to attend the meeting in Aspen include: Robert F. Chase, Henry Cisneros, Nancy Cole, Ervin Duggan, John S. Hendricks, Ron Kirk, Gerald Levin, Sol Trujillo, and Raul Yzaguirre.

Prior to the annual meeting of FOCAS CEOs, a preparatory session was held in April 1998 at the Wye River Conference Centers in Maryland. There, designated representatives of FOCAS members and additional experts helped us understand better the issue of information literacy and design an agenda for the annual meeting. We sincerely value the contributions of the following attendees at the preparatory session (a complete list, with organizational affiliations, appears in the appendix): Peter Bankson, John Buffalo, Harold C. Crump, Michael Eisenberg, Maggi G. Gaines, Doris McCarter, Virginia Gehr McEnerney, Bernadette McGuire-Rivera, David Morse, John Orlando, Nancy Pelz-Paget, Andrew S. Petersen, Marilyn Reznick, Arthur Sheekey, and Timothy Walter.

We are especially indebted to Patricia Senn Breivik, Dean of Libraries at Wayne State University and chair of the National Forum on Information Literacy, for her work as a consultant to the 1998 FOCAS and her preparation of a comprehensive background paper on information literacy which appears in the appendix to this report. Finally, we thank Richard Adler, conference rapporteur, for once again producing an interesting and informative report of the FOCAS meeting. We wish to acknowledge the work of Elizabeth Golder for her coordination of both the Preparatory Session and the Aspen conference, Sunny Sumter for the production of this publication, copy editor David Stearman, and Melanie Turner for the cover design and layout.

Charles M. Firestone
Executive Vice President, Policy Programs
and
Executive Director, Communications and Society Program
The Aspen Institute

Amy Korzick Garmer
Associate Director, Communications and Society Program
The Aspen Institute

Information Literacy: Advancing Opportunities for Learning in the Digital Age

Introduction

"It is the best of wires, and the worst of wires."

The foregoing paraphrase of Dickens was how one participant in the Aspen Institute's 1998 Forum on Communications and Society (FOCAS) summed up the current state and impact of the Internet. On one hand, the Internet has provided more people with more convenient access to more information in a shorter period of time than any other medium in history. It has given rise to an enormous burst of entrepreneurial activity that has led to the creation of an entire new industry in just a few years. Electronic commerce already is a multibillion dollar enterprise and will become even more important in the near future.

On the other hand, not all citizens enjoy the benefits of the Internet equally. Approximately one-third of American adults now have access to the Internet, according to the most recent surveys. Not surprisingly, people who are younger, more affluent, and better educated tend to be online, whereas those who are older, economically disadvantaged, less well-educated, or live in rural areas of the country are less likely to be online. This discrepancy has created what has been called a "digital divide" that threatens to widen the gap between the information "haves" and "have nots" in our society.

Even among people who are online, the Internet has been a mixed blessing. Because the Internet evolved so rapidly, there are few guideposts that allow us to navigate confidently through an overabundance of information. It is easy to become disoriented and overwhelmed by the plethora of competing sources. Moreover, because the Internet is an open medium, with few mechanisms to filter or evaluate what gets put online, it provides a forum for content of all kinds—factual and fallacious, genuine and fraudulent, positive and negative, helpful and pernicious. With no gatekeepers to take responsibility for the quality of content, individual users must figure out what to make of the information they find. As online usage grows, so do concerns about issues such as fraud and invasion of users' privacy.

The starting point for the 1998 FOCAS meeting was the recognition that this new networked world poses new challenges to individuals and to society and that new initiatives may be required to ensure that its benefits outweigh its costs.

An Exploding Universe

Eric Schmidt, chairman and chief executive officer (CEO) of Novell and co-chair of the 1998 FOCAS, opened the meeting by trying to provide a sense of the reach of the Internet and the pace at which it is growing. He asserted that the Internet has grown faster than all other technologies that preceded it. The number of people connected to the Internet worldwide has grown from 3 million people in 1994 to more than 100 million today. According to the most recent Nielsen/CommerceNet survey, 79 million Americans over age 16—or 35 percent of the adult population— are now using the Internet. The total volume of traffic carried on the Internet already is greater than 1,000 terabytes per month and is doubling every 100 days.

Even as the Internet's penetration continues to grow, its fundamental nature continues to evolve. New types of software are being developed to provide new services and new kinds of functionality. The World Wide Web is evolving from a collection of static pages to dynamic sites that support a variety of transactions and other types of interactivity. Internet-based virtual communities are emerging in which people with common interests are able to find one another and exchange information and conduct business with each other. Virtually all large enterprises—from IBM and Dell Computer to L.L. Bean and Godiva Chocolates—and thousands of smaller ones are establishing online presences. As electronic commerce (e-commerce) grows, companies are restructuring themselves to connect directly with customers who may be anywhere in the world.

The way people access the Internet also is changing. Although most residential users currently get online by means of relatively slow dial-up connections (a maximum of 56.6 kilobits per second), many users are in the process of moving toward accessing the Internet through high-speed digital networks that will be "always on, always aware." The network will be available through wireless connections as well as through conventional wires. In addition to personal computers, many households will soon be equipped with home networks and inexpensive "set-top boxes" that provide access to the Internet as well as to digital television programming. In a world of ubiquitous connectivity, we will be able to be online wherever we are and whatever we are doing; we will be able to get access to the information we want and to send and receive messages instantly to anyone else online.

These new technologies, Schmidt asserted, are forming the basis for a new society that we don't yet fully understand. Michael Jordan, CEO of CBS, agreed that we are living in an "exploding universe" that is fundamentally new and different. As technology continues to evolve, its effects will continue to expand as well. The impacts are being felt in economic, personal, and political realms.

On the economic front, we continue to move into an increasingly intensive information economy. U.S. Rep. Edward Markey (D-Mass.) pointed out that with the passage of the General Agreement on Trade and Tariffs (GATT) and the North American Free Trade Agreement (NAFTA), the United States committed itself to competing in a global marketplace. As a result, the number of manufacturing jobs will continue to decline; new jobs will require greater intelligence, knowledge, and the ability to use information effectively. Whatever skills one has now, it is very likely that it will be necessary to continue to acquire new skills throughout one's career to remain employable.[1] Education and the ability to function effectively in an intensely competitive, continuously changing marketplace will become increasingly critical.

In our personal lives, the new media provide a greater array of choices, but they also require greater discrimination and new skills to use them appropriately. Whereas traditional media such as television and print provide structured, prepackaged experiences, the Internet invites us to "jump in and play." The new environment is interactive, dynamic, and decentralized and makes less distinction than older media between consumers and producers of content. In a world of electronic virtual communities, one's identity and reputation are based on how one expresses oneself and how well one can interact with others. To be effective in this environment, we need to know the rules of the game and have the chips to play in it.

In addition, as online commerce continues to expand, citizens will need to understand how to shop in virtual stores, conduct electronic transactions effectively, guard against fraud, and protect their privacy.

Finally, technology is creating new challenges for citizens in the political realm. As media outlets proliferate, so does the volume of political discourse. The new media provide a mixture of objective reporting and subjective commentary, nonpartisan analysis and partisan argument, authoritative pronouncements and unsubstantiated rumor. According to the late political scientist Robert A. Dahl, "The scale, complexity, and sheer volume of information impose ever stronger demands on the capacities of citizens."[2] In other words, individuals must sort through the masses of information available to them and reach their own conclusions.

Former Federal Communications Commission (FCC) chairman Reed Hundt, co-chair of the 1998 FOCAS, summarized the social impacts of technology by asserting that it is:

- inevitable;
- disintermediating;
- value-shaping;
- extending (our senses);
- problem-creating; and
- solution-generating.

AT&T CEO Michael Armstrong responded by claiming that, increasingly, "The Internet is society."

The question that the 1998 FOCAS meeting attempted to answer was, What are the competencies that will be required to be successful in this new environment? More specifically, what do we need to do as a society to prepare the students of today to live and work in this rapidly emerging networked world?

What is Information Literacy?

Traditionally, one of the most fundamental goals of schooling has been to ensure that students are literate—that is, able to read and to write. There was no disagreement among FOCAS participants that these two abilities, along with the third "R"—Arithmetic—remain the core skills that education must provide to all students. However, the participants agreed that these skills are no longer enough. Beyond the basic ability to read and write, other kinds of "literacies" have been proposed as vital for effective functioning today:

- *Computer literacy.* Because of the central role of the computer as a tool for accessing and processing information, a great deal of emphasis has been placed on providing students with access to computers in their education. Computer literacy is generally understood as a familiarity with computing concepts and the ability to use common applications such as word processors, databases, and spreadsheets. In some cases, computer literacy is considered to include the ability to write programs, at least on a basic level.

  American schools have made a significant investment in providing students with access to computers. In 1998, the ratio of students to computers in U.S. elementary and secondary schools was approximately 7 to 1—a dramatic improvement from a ratio of 32 to 1 a decade earlier.[3] Yet many educators believe that more needs to be done not only to provide wider access to computers but to ensure that they are used properly. For example, a recent study found that only 6 percent of elementary and secondary classroom "fully integrate technology"; 54 percent of schools have outdated and inadequate technology.[4]

- *Technical literacy.* This capability has been defined as "the ability to apply mathematics and the sciences to the solution of a physical problem or the realization of new products."[5] Ever since the Soviet Union launched Sputnik in 1957, Americans have worried about the ability of students to master technical skills and help build a high-tech workforce. International tests that have compared the performance of U.S. students in math and science with those of students in other countries have generally found American students at or near the bottom of the rankings. There also is evidence suggesting that U.S. schools are not producing enough technically trained graduates to satisfy the needs of industry. In recent years, high-tech companies have lobbied vigorously to expand the annual quota of visas to allow a larger number of foreign workers with technical skills into the country to take jobs that would otherwise go unfilled because of a shortage of Americans with the requisite skills.

- *Digital literacy.* Some observers have begun to argue that the new information environment created by the Internet requires students to master a distinctively new set of skills to function effectively. The Internet represents such a radically different way to present, access, and use information that the ability to make productive use of the resources it offers requires new skills. For example, an instructor in Web design has expressed concern that "kids [may] know how to read, but not how to do [a] systematic search for information, to critically approach and assess a medium" such as the World Wide Web.[6] Another Internet expert has argued that students need to learn new ways of expressing themselves: "As soon as children go beyond nursery rhymes, we want to start having them develop Web sites instead of writing reports and essays."[7]

From this perspective, schools need to provide students with more than simply access to computers; they must provide access to computers that are linked to the Internet. Educators and community leaders have been working hard to wire their schools, and the percentage of public schools with access to the Internet has climbed from 35 percent in 1994 to 78 percent in 1997.[8] However, detailed information about how computers and the Internet are actually being used in the schools remains scarce.

Participants in the FOCAS meeting took note of all of these different types of literacies. They concluded that these specific skills are included in the broader term *information literacy.*

There was a lively debate among FOCAS participants about just what constitutes information literacy. Some participants argued that technology is evolving so rapidly and is bringing with it such fundamental changes in what it means to be information literate that there is little point in trying to pin down an explicit definition.

Because of this rapid change, it is risky to link the definition of literacy too closely to any specific technology. Not very long ago, for example, the ability to use a computer was generally understood to include the ability to program it. Today, most computer users have little need to do their own programming. Similarly, with the development of graphical user interfaces (first introduced to personal computers by Apple Macintosh, then popularized by Microsoft Windows), the need to master the arcane commands of an operating system have become far less important for the average user.

Although technology is extremely important, there is a danger of focusing on it too much. As Lord Briggs, former chancellor of Britain's Open University, pointed out, "We will make a serious mistake if we think that the only thing that matters in society is technology or that the future of society rests on technology." Governor Michael Leavitt of Utah agreed, noting that "we can get overzealous in promoting technology" as the solution to all of our problems.

FCC chairman William Kennard cautioned that we should resist the temptation to define too specifically what technology is and what it can do. In fact, we don't know how technology will evolve and how it will be used in the future. What we need to do is to ensure that everyone has equal access to technology, then allow them to determine for themselves how they will use it.

There was a general consensus about what information literacy should include. John Doerr, a partner at the venture capital firm of Kleiner Perkins Caufield & Byers, suggested that there are four components of information literacy that encompass a broad range of skills:

- the ability to read;
- the ability to publish one's views;
- the ability to manipulate symbols; and
- the ability to think critically and independently.

The first three of these abilities are similar to the "3 R's." The fourth is becoming increasingly important in a networked world. Jolynn Barry Butler, president of the National Association of Regulatory Utility Commissioners, noted that we need to find ways to "get kids to think critically about the information they are accessing: Is it good, bad, objective, or biased? If we are putting computers in the hands of five- and six-year-olds, then we need to start teaching critical thinking skills at an earlier age than we used to."

Several participants felt that any definition of information literacy should include an emphasis on values. Ira Fishman, former CEO of the Schools and Libraries Corporation, argued that while we are teaching students to understand and manipulate symbols, we need to impart "substantive norms" to ensure that they are able to set positive goals for themselves and distinguish right from wrong. Zoë Baird, president of the John and Mary R. Markle Foundation, agreed that there must be a "value component to literacy" because information is not value-free—nor are the media. Therefore, we need to help students develop their own set of values that will guide their judgments about what they see and hear.

One important reason for stressing the values components of "info-literacy" is that as a society we need to come to grips with the implications of the wired world that is rapidly coming into existence. If war is too important to leave to the generals, technology is too important to leave entirely to the technologists. Rebecca Rimel, president of the Pew Charitable Trusts, asserted that "we used to have an understanding of the collective good, but we don't have it anymore. As we unleash the new technologies, we need to think how they can be harnessed without destroying our communities."

Information Literacy and the Schools

One point that received universal agreement from FOCAS participants is that the nation's schools need to do a better job of producing students who are information literate. Mayor Kurt Schmoke of Baltimore asserted that the quality of the schools in his city is still "a central issue" for him. Michael Leavitt agreed, adding that he worries that the schools are not doing a good enough job of equipping students to "know what they need to know."

The public K-12 school system in the United States is a massive enterprise. As of the fall of 1997, there were 51 million students enrolled in 87,200 schools employing more than 2.5 million teachers. If one were to add together the budgets of all public school systems across the country, the collective annual budget would be approximately $350 billion.[9]

If schools are to do a better job of preparing students for a future rich with information and digital technologies, educators, government officials, and community leaders will have to address several fundamental issues that affect the quality of the learning experience. These issues include the teaching of basic skills, the role of technology in learning, teacher preparation and training, the structure and organization of schools, the need for lifelong learning, and the role of families in their children's education.

Teaching Basic Skills

Many FOCAS participants, including Michael Armstrong and Children's Television Workshop CEO David Britt, asserted that the ability to read is still "absolutely fundamental" for any other kind of literacy. Lord Briggs concurred, noting that the ability to read provides the essential foundation for all later learning.

Several participants cited promising programs that have been developed to improve the teaching of reading—and the barriers they face in being adopted on a wider basis. For example, Mayor Schmoke described his city's experience with a program called "Writing to Read" developed by IBM. This program was initially introduced to 5,000 first and second graders in the Baltimore schools. When the students were tested, they showed dramatic improvements in their reading abilities. Schmoke then pushed to expand the program, but the teachers disliked it (presumably because it was based on the intensive use of computers), and the state school board failed to support it. It ended up as a "two-year fad."

The Role of Technology in Learning

Although technology has an important role to play in improving education, there is still considerable disagreement about its proper role in the schools. As Lois Jean White, president of the National PTA, observed, "Wiring up the schools is a good thing, but they need much more than that." After years of effort and billions of dollars spent equipping U.S. schools with computers and connecting them to the Internet, evidence for a payoff from the investment remains scanty. One reason is that there has been relatively little systematic evaluation of the effectiveness of computers and technology in education. The evidence that is available suggests that technology can improve learning but that it is not a "magic bullet."

For example, a recent study of student performance in mathematics (one of the first based on national test data) did find a significant relationship between math scores among fourth and eighth graders and their use of computers. Among fourth graders, students who had used computers for math and learning games scored better than those who had not. Among eighth graders, students who used computers for mathematical simulations and applications scored better than those who did not use computers. At the same time, eighth graders whose use of computers was confined to more basic drill and practice in math actually scored lower than students with no access to computers.[10]

Teacher Preparation and Training

The study cited above also found that students in both grades whose teachers had received training in the educational use of computers did better than students with teachers without training. FOCAS participants recognized that the quality of instruction that students receive remains the most important factor in the quality of their education. Some participants worried that too many teachers are still unfamiliar and uncomfortable with technology and are unprepared to provide the kind of instruction required to make students information literate. As Mayor Schmoke observed, "Students may understand why they need new skills, but their teachers don't."

Rep. Markey added that the problem may run even deeper. He noted that in Massachusetts, half of the new applicants for teaching jobs in elementary and secondary schools failed a basic competency test. Governor Leavitt added that when Colorado set a minimum standard for teachers, half of the teachers in the state fell below it. A recent report from the National Commission on Teaching and America's Future concluded that as many as 75 percent of the country's teachers are not "fully qualified" for their jobs.[11]

A looming shortage of elementary and secondary school teachers offers an opportunity and a challenge for improving the overall quality of public education. Because of a projected increase of three million students in the overall public school population by 2007 and the retirement of many current teachers, two million new teachers will have to be trained and hired over the next decade. The question is whether this turnover will be seized as an opportunity to upgrade and modernize the skills of the nation's teachers—or whether school districts will resort to cutting corners and lowering standards to meet their hiring needs. School districts in states such as California have already hired new teachers without the normal teaching credentials in response to an increase in student populations and mandated decreases in maximum classroom size.

Structure and Organization of Schools

An equally important question is whether the schools as they are currently organized can provide the kind of educational experiences that students need to succeed in an information society. Some of the FOCAS participants believed that the educational system requires fundamental restructuring if it is to remain effective. Michael Jordan noted that to remain competitive in a rapidly changing world, businesses have shifted from a traditional top-down, "command and control" structure to a more flexible structure based on autonomous teams. The educational system may need to go through a similar transformation that puts less emphasis on the teacher as the primary source of knowledge for students and more on a model in which teachers and students work together to solve problems and find answers to questions. In this model, the fact that some students may be more adept at using technology than their teachers is less of a threat to the teacher's authority and more of an opportunity for productive collaboration.

In addition, computer technology has the ability to provide each student with resources and learning experiences that are custom tailored to his or her particular level and learning style. Martin Ernst, research affiliate at the Harvard Program on Information Resources Policy, pointed out that computers can be powerful "teaching machines" that get students excited and enhance their learning. Reed Hundt stated that computer and communications technologies "allow for a profound change in the educational model." They can open the classroom to resources anywhere in the world, allow for much greater individualization of education (which Governor Leavitt described as "menu-driven education"), and make it easier to gather and disseminate data on student and school performance. Most schools and classrooms are not currently set up to use educational technologies effectively, however.

Technology can also be used to provide access to opportunities for learning that are completely decoupled from the formal institutions of schools. Peter Price, president of Television USA, commented that, high-quality education has been treated as "a controlled substance," where "the best stuff was available only at the fancy schools." Now, as a result of the proliferation of educational software and online learning resources, traditional barriers to education are—at least in theory—disappearing. Computers are already in 50 percent of U.S. households and nearly two-thirds of households with children. As John Doerr pointed out, cable companies are beginning to deploy "set-top computers" that will provide high-speed Internet access as well as digital television. Within a few years, these devices should be available wherever cable is, creating an infrastructure capable of delivering high-quality education directly to a majority of households.

Lifelong Learning

No matter how good students' initial education may be, they will almost certainly continue to need to learn new information and new skills throughout their careers. U.S. corporations already spend more than $55 billion annually on formal training (approximately $420 per worker per year).[12] As the pace of change accelerates, the importance of ongoing training on and off the job will continue to increase. What the educational system must do is ensure that all students "learn to learn" while they are in school so that they can keep themselves current as new technologies emerge.

Role of Families

Finally, although the quality of the instruction in the schools is extremely important, FOCAS participants recognized that families have a role of equal or greater importance in determining students' achievements. As Michael Jordan noted, it is "parents who have the greatest potential impact on children's ability to learn." Governor Leavitt agreed, observing that "there does not seem to be a direct connection between money invested in schools and results. What matters most is the extent of family involvement."

New Initiatives

After grappling with the challenge of defining information literacy and discussing the crucial role of schools, FOCAS participants turned their attention to identifying collaborative actions and specific initiatives to improve the level of information literacy in society. The initiatives proposed by FOCAS members are summarized below.

These initiatives could be further developed and implemented—by FOCAS members or others—to further the goal of an "info-literate" citizenry. In some instances, FOCAS members already are pursuing individual proposals. This list is by no means exhaustive; many other projects could enhance efforts to improve opportunities and outcomes for greater information literacy. These initiatives do represent a good start, however.

Initiative 1: Promote Greater Awareness of Information Literacy

FOCAS members recognize that the concept of information literacy is unfamiliar to most citizens—perhaps even to most educators. The first task, therefore, is to create an awareness of the importance of information literacy skills as the capability to deal with the ever-expanding reach of technology and information in every facet of society. These skills include the ability to read, to identify important questions and be able to find their answers, to manipulate symbols (both qualitative and quantitative), to think critically and independently, and to communicate effectively through a variety of media.

Several FOCAS participants suggested the creation of a national commission to explore the social significance of the Internet and other new technologies in a civil society. The commission would explore issues such as access to technology, the economics of information, and the role of values in guiding the development of technology. The work of the commission would contribute to a broader awareness of the importance of information literacy and an understanding of what it entails.

Initiative 2: Assess and Hold Educators and Political Leaders at All Levels Accountable for Students' Proficiency in Information Literacy

If information literacy is a critical skill, we need ways to measure it. In particular, we need to establish mechanisms to assess how well our educational system is doing in providing students with information literacy skills—and then hold educational and political leaders accountable for the results.

FOCAS participants strongly supported the development of quantitative performance standards in academic areas such as reading and math that would provide feedback on how well schools are doing. Although there was relatively little enthusiasm for mandatory national standards, there was considerable support for a set of voluntary standards that would provide a measure of our success in equipping students with the skills they need and create pressure for schools to make sure their students are adequately educated. (There was some disagreement whether a uniform set of national standards was preferable to standards set by each state. Governor Leavitt noted that 38 states have already established educational standards, but the standards differ from state to state.)

Once standards are established, information about how well schools are doing in preparing students to meet the standards should be made available to the public. The Internet itself represents a powerful tool for disseminating data about the performance of individual schools. In California, for example, a new Web-based organization called Great Schools has been set up to offer access to profiles on public schools in Silicon Valley, including student performance on statewide standardized tests. Initially, the site includes about 100 schools that have agreed to provide information about themselves, but the organization hopes eventually to provide data on more than 1,000 schools in the area.

A related proposal calls for community media such as newspapers and radio and television stations in each market to review local schools in much the same way they now review plays, films, and restaurants. Shining a spotlight on successes can be as effective as (and less threatening than) calling attention to failures. Publishing and promoting best practices in education can help spread the word about what is working and encourage others to adopt those practices in their schools.

Finally, several proposals were made to create independent mechanisms that would allow individuals to test their own abilities and certify their accomplishments. Mark Warner, managing director of Columbia Capital, has proposed the establishment of an Information Technology Certification Exam that would enable college students, including those in nontechnical fields, to document their knowledge of and aptitude for using computers. Warner is now heading an effort to introduce such a test in Virginia under the auspices of the state's Foundation for Independent Colleges.

Initiative 3: Give Teachers the Preparation and Support They Need To Do a Better Job

The need to recruit and train more than two million new public school teachers within the next decade will provide an unprecedented opportunity to enhance and update the skills of the country's educators. An urgent task is to include a strong emphasis on information literacy skills in the training that these new teachers receive. The deans of the country's schools of education can play a key role in making sure that information literacy is part of the curriculum of their institutions. At the same time, credentialing requirements for teachers should include competence in using technology.

Programs must be developed to familiarize teachers with the technological tools available to them and to help them keep up with the rapidly changing information environment in which their students live. Information literacy also should be included in continuing education requirements for teachers already in classrooms, as well as for those who will be joining them in the future.

In addition, new initiatives are needed to enable teachers to connect more easily with peers in their communities and elsewhere to support one another and share successful teaching strategies. Many Web sites provide access to useful educational content and to information about innovative approaches to teaching. These sites need to be supported and promoted.

James Barr, president and CEO of TDS Telecom, described a program his company has initiated to identify and support "technology champions" in schools in communities in which his company operates. These teachers or administrators are given special training and part-time summer jobs to familiarize themselves with new technology tools. Then they are sent out to other schools and other districts to share what they have learned. William Milliken, president of Communities In Schools, described a similar program that his organization is launching in partnership with Cisco Systems to identify and support "youth champions" in 1,000 schools across the country whose responsibilities will include promoting the effective uses of technology.

Initiative 4: Involve Parents More Deeply in Their Children's Education

Schools need to be connected with and supported by their communities, and parents need to take more responsibility for their children's education. A number of recommendations focused on strategies for bringing schools and their communities closer together.

Mayor Schmoke argued that parents need to be empowered to have an impact on their children's education, not merely informed about what is going on in their schools. They need to have some way to influence their children's education and to have some choice in the kind of education their children receive.

Information technology can play a useful role in enhancing links between school and home. Many schools already have Web sites that provide places for students to display their work. These sites could be expanded to provide data that parents could use to evaluate a school's performance (for example, data on the results of standardized tests).

John Doerr argued that the most important wiring in the schools is that which will connect teachers directly to the parents of their students. He called for programs to equip teachers with cell phones and voice mailboxes that would allow them to communicate easily with the parents of their students.

Another proposal was to create an online mechanism for student "self-certification." If standardized tests were available on the Internet, students and their families could gauge their progress in core subjects such as reading and math.

Employers also need to get involved more actively in working to improve the quality of education in the communities in which they operate. If schools fail to prepare students adequately for the workforce, the result is not merely an educational crisis but a business crisis. Many businesses already have formed partnerships with local schools to provide resources needed by the schools and to offer rewards to students who excel academically. Businesses can do more, however, to focus attention on the specific skills that students will need to get and hold good jobs. For example, employers in local communities could require new employees to pass a competency test in information literacy.

Initiative 5: Develop a Dramatically Different Technology-based Educational Alternative

A particularly interesting proposal from FOCAS participants was an initiative intended to dramatize the limitations of the current educational system and the need for new models. This initiative would create a new Internet-based educational institution that would provide a complete high school education. Mayor Schmoke proposed that this new institution—to be known as the Baltimore Elementary and Secondary Technology School, or the BEST school—be based in his city.

Following the Aspen meeting, a working group began to explore how this program should be developed. According to the initial proposal developed by the group:

- BEST would be a free online high school with a state-of-the-art, interactive curriculum. It would be available to qualified high school students and would be accredited by the State of Maryland. It would provide an alternative means of earning a Maryland high school diploma—making it an attractive alternative to nontraditional students, dropouts, and parents who are seeking an alternative to underperforming schools in their own neighborhoods.

- BEST would provide more alternatives in education for young people. It would function as an independent public school online. A governing board consisting of business and community leaders, educators, and others would manage it. The curriculum would be designed by educators, with input from the business community.

- The design of BEST would allow students to work independently, as well as allowing clusters of students to work together in association with a community group or organization. Service learning would be a component of the program, as would association with a mentor. In addition, students would be encouraged to pursue a range of extracurricular activities in association with schools as well as independently. Students would need to meet as a learning community for a minimum of six hours weekly to qualify for a State of Maryland high school diploma.

Initiative 6: Increase Funding for Research in Education and Information Literacy

Spending on research designed to evaluate and improve the effectiveness of education currently represents approximately 0.1 percent of total expenditures on education.[13] This figure contrasts with typical expenditures of 5–10 percent of annual revenues for research and development at typical companies and as much as 20–25 percent at some high-tech companies.

More research is urgently needed on the effectiveness of various teaching methods, including technology-based techniques; alternative models for education; and various approaches to curriculum development. Longer-term studies are also needed to track the success of students over time in different educational programs.

Conclusion

Perhaps the greatest immediate challenge for the diffusion of information literacy skills is to create a level playing field for access to technology. More should be done to ensure that the digital divide between the information haves and have-nots does not widen further. The "E-Rate" program mandated by Congress and implemented by the FCC is currently collecting more than $1 billion annually from telephone companies and allocating the money to schools and libraries to purchase computers and online access. Schools in rural areas and in poorer communities continue to lag behind those in more affluent areas in their ability to provide all students with access to technology, however.

Policymakers and business and community leaders must work together to search for ways to improve opportunities and outcomes for learning and enhanced information literacy for all members of society. The FOCAS encourages all stakeholders to join these efforts to identify workable solutions to the challenge of information literacy as we prepare to enter the 21st century.

Notes

1. See Richard Adler, *Jobs, Technology and Employability*, (Queenstown, Md.: The Aspen Institute, 1998).

2. Robert A. Dahl, "The Problem of Civic Competence," in *Toward Democracy: A Journey* (Berkeley, Ca.: Institute of Governmental Studies Press, 1977), p. 219.

3. *School Technology and Readiness Report*—Year 2 (Washington, D.C.: CEO Forum on Education and Technology), February 22, 1999, p. 24. This quantitative assessment of the status of computers in U.S. schools, though a useful gauge of progress, does not reveal important information about the age or functional capability of those computers and thus should be used with a measure of caution.

4. *School Technology and Readiness Report*—Year 2, p. 13.

5. Constantine N. Anagnostopoulos and Lauren A. Williams, "Few Gold Stars for Pre-College Education," *IEEE Spectrum*, April 1988, p. 20.

6. Linda M. Castellitto, "To Some, It's Never Too Early to Teach Web 101," *Internet World*, September 28, 1998, p. 36.

7. Ibid.

8. *School Technology and Readiness Report*—Year 2, p.26.

9. Anagnostopoulos and Williams, "Few Gold Stars for Pre-College Education," pp. 19–20.

10. Jeff Archer, "The Link to Higher Test Scores," *Education Week Online*, October 1998, <www.edweek.org/sreports/tc98>.

11. Fully qualified teachers are defined as having studied child development, and learning and teaching methods, holding degrees in the subject areas they teach, and having passed state license requirements. National Commission on Teaching and America's Future, *What Matters Most: Teaching for America's Future* (Washington, D.C., 1998).

12. Adler, *Jobs, Technology, and Employability*, p. 27.

13. "Technology Counts '98–Putting School Technology To The Test," *Education Week Online*, October 1998, <www.edweek.org/sreports/tc98>.

APPENDIX

Information Literacy
Background Paper

Introduction

The arrival of the postindustrial information society was loudly and repeatedly announced in the 1970s and 1980s. Many observers hoped that the Information Age would contribute to the solution of many longstanding problems and that it would lessen the gap between haves and have-nots. As early as 1970, however, the not so friendly side of an information-rich society was becoming evident. Alvin Toffler wrote of "information overload,"[1] and by 1989 Richard Saul Wurman was describing the outcome of information overload: "information anxiety."[2] Corporate leaders, meanwhile, were also being warned that "the only thing as difficult and dangerous as managing a large enterprise with too little information is managing one with too much."[3]

A sampling of statistics since then reveals the extent to which information overload is a legitimate concern:

- The total number of U.S. copyright registrations made in 1996 was 550,400; the number of registrations in 1997 was projected by the copyright office to exceed 560,000.[4]

- In addition to the 10,616 newspapers in circulation in the United States in 1996, there were more than 4,100 World Wide Web-based news sites operating according to professional journalistic standards. More than 1,600 of these sites are operated by companies that also produce printed newspapers.[5]

- The number of newspapers in daily circulation worldwide increased from 8,206 in 1990 to 9,315 in 1992.[6]

- New book titles published in the United States jumped from 46,738 in 1990 to more than 62,000 in 1995.[7]

- 1.7 billion dollars are spent annually on corporate libraries; 70,000 people are employed in them.[8]

- More than 100,000 U.S. federal and more than 10,000 United Nations documents are produced annually; no one knows how many state and local documents also pour out.

  In addition to the very real explosion of information, use of information technology is changing how business is conducted—though whether for better or for worse is far from clear.

- The number of small businesses (100 employees or fewer) that will have networked personal computers will rise to nearly 12 million in 1999.[9]

- 55 percent of all employees now use computing technology; 70 percent are connected to a local area network.[10]

- An international survey documented that scholars spend approximately 44 percent of their office hours (based on 45-hour week) working on the Internet and 56 percent on paper-based and face-to-face activities.[11]

- Little to no change in business productivity appears to result from major investments in information systems.

- Business leaders question the value of much of the time employees spend "surfing" the Internet.[12]

Why? What is the cause of so little progress from the high investments made in technology and the accompanying exponentially expanding information base in America? Why have the hopes for lessening the gap between the haves and have-nots in the Information Age remained so elusive?

The Lure of the Quick Fix

At least part of this dilemma can be seen as the flip side to America's strong suit: our Yankee know-how and love of a quick fix. Somehow, better mousetraps and now better computers and networks always seem to hold the promise of solving our people problems: our education problems, our workforce problems, and our societal problems. Each wave of new technology is heralded as the dawn of a new and better millenium and each in its turn fails to meet hoped for outcomes. To reap better outcomes from our technology investments, a national reevaluation of our country's almost exclusive focus on technology will be required. At the local and national levels and in school and business settings, the emphasis must be placed on empowering people. People must be empowered not only to use technology well but also to effectively evaluate and use the information to which technology provides access. As one group of national leaders has stated "Technology alone will never allow America to reach the potential inherent in the Information Age... [T]he dreams of a new and better tomorrow will only begin to be realized when all young people graduate into the workforce with strong information literacy skills."[13]

What is Information Literacy?

It may be best to start building a definition of information literacy by determining what it is not. It is not:

- library literacy
- media literacy
- computer literacy
- network or Internet literacy
- technology literacy

Information literacy encompasses all of these types of literacy, but is more than the sum of all of them. Even more importantly, the focus of information literacy is different from all of these literacies in one very significant aspect. Whereas the specific literacies focus on learning about things, information literacy focuses on people's empowerment for success in today's information-rich society. Information literacy starts with people who have a problem or need to make a decision (whether in their personal or professional lives) and incorporates all of the abilities they need to effectively access and use information to address their needs. In this setting, the other literacies become tools for achieving desired outcomes.

The most widely used definition of information literacy was promulgated in the *ALA Presidential Report on Information Literacy: Final Report*. That report defines information literacy as follows:

- knowing when information is needed;
- identifying the information needed to address a given problem or issue;
- finding the needed information;
- organizing the needed information; and
- using the information effectively to address the problem or issue at hand.[14]

Computer/Technology Literacy vs. Information Literacy

Currently far more attention is being paid nationally and on campuses to computer or technology literacy than to information literacy. The National Research Council's Computer Science and Telecommunications Board general education curriculum requirements on many campuses, suggests that many people appear to believe that being able to understand and use computers is the fundamental need of the workforce today.

On the other hand, in a special report funded by the Milken Family Foundation entitled "Learning in a Digital Age: Insights into the Issues," Kathleen Fulton, associate director of the Center for Learning and Educational Technology, underscores the information literacy imperative over other literacies:

> Concern about information literacy predates the computer age. In language arts, there has long been an emphasis on teaching students to develop skills they need in order to analyze the written word and the messages found therein. With the growing influence of television in our daily lives, many have called for media literacy that gives students tools to interpret, critique, and evaluate what they see on television and in movies and videos. However, today's rapid growth of the Internet and the access it provides to large amounts of information has ignited a firestorm of concern regarding the need for increased attention to information literacy. Unlike the information students receive from earlier forms of media (textbooks, television, documentaries,

and library materials) all of which have been carefully researched, documented, and selected for publication and presentation, especially when used in educational settings—what comes across on the Internet is "undigested" information, provided by expert and novice alike, scholars and shysters, pedagogues and pedophiles. The days when teachers and parents were able to control and orchestrate all the information presented to students are past. The technology pull of the Internet will force the issue of developing broader information literacy skills for all students if we expect them to sort the wheat from the chaff, the true from the untrue, the rumor from the real.[15]

One expert in end-user computing systems and training makes clear distinctions among computer, information, and information technology literacies:

Computer Literacy. Although it's a popular term, the requisite skills are often understated. It means that an individual possesses the necessary keyboard skills and hardware and software knowledge to use applications correctly, has a good understanding of computer hardware and software capabilities and limitations, and is skilled at exploiting computers to help accomplish information-based tasks.

Information Literacy. It's often confused with computer literacy, but it requires a different set of skills. Information literacy implies that an individual be able to determine when information is needed and define the information needs in searchable terms. He/she is familiar with the vast array of information resources available and proficient at accessing and using them to locate desired information.

Information Technology Literacy. This literacy requires a different knowledge base from the other two. It purports that an individual is familiar with current information technologies, such as digital electronics, optical data storage, advanced computers, and artificial intelligence.

He/she understands what the latest developments are within these technologies, knows how these developments are changing the competitive world, and realizes how these developments can be innovatively applied.[16]

Insofar as a country is technology rich, computer and technology literacies are prerequisites for information literacy—much as the ability to read is a prerequisite. Neither, however, should be seen as an end in itself any more than the ability to read is of value apart from a person's having access to printed information that is wanted or needed. Indeed, one could well make the case for information literacy as the final component in any adult literacy program.

How Do Students Develop Information Literacy Abilities?

One way to ensure that students develop information literacy abilities is to have all the key players (teachers, students, school administrators, and parents) agree on how an information-literate student will perform. Possibly the best such statement, soon to be officially released, is the result of a joint development project by the American Association of School Librarians and the Association for Educational Communications and Technology.[17]

Resource-Based Learning

Today's schools and campuses are undertaking many approaches to try to move teachers from being the "sage on the stage" to being the "guide on the side," thus creating a more dynamic learning environment that will produce more active learning. The terminology used for such efforts varies from setting to setting. Some of the most frequently used terms are inquiry learning, problem-based learning, evidence-based learning, undergraduate research, and resource-based learning. The latter term particularly recognizes that if students are to continue to learn throughout their lives, they must be able to access, evaluate, organize, and present information from all of the sources existing in today's information society. Such sources include books, journals, television, online databases, radio, community experts, government agencies, the Internet, and CD-ROM's. As a result, all of these resources become learning tools. Resource-based learning discourages a blind faith in information sources and emphasizes the importance of learning how to evaluate and effectively use information over merely finding the information. Thereasa Wesley, coordinator of instructional services at Northern Kentucky University, describes this concept as follows:

> Primarily we want to teach students that scholars and authorities do disagree and that this is a positive catalyst to the creation of new knowledge. A discussion of conflicts among scholars will probably be surprising to students. Much of the educational process docs not make this lack of complete consensus evident: single instructors for a class, straight lecture classes, single texts—all summary type sources that take the edge off the controversy and varying interpretations of any issue.

> Secondly, we can show them that factual information is fluid and can change due to its context. For example, some reports claim plastics make up 30 percent of the landfill while others claim only 8 percent. Which is true? Why is there a difference? Investigation of the sources cited in these reports indicates that one source is discussing volume, the other weight. Students should know the context of facts before using them in their own analysis of an issue.

> Finally, we should try to build students' confidence in their ability to question and judge the value, relevancy, accuracy, bias, etc., of these information sources.[18]

Resource-based learning is equally effective in the school setting, as the following example illustrates.

> *The Titanic.* To begin this unit, the teacher and the library media specialist present the following question: "What would have made the outcome of the Titanic disaster different?" As students work on finding the

answer to this question, they cover material from many different subject areas. In math, for example, the sixth graders figure out such problems as the number of lifeboats available to the passengers and the distance between the Titanic and the rescue ship. For science, they study glaciers and displacement. For social studies, they look at social issues of the times that dictated class status and determined who got to abandon the ship first. Before writing an expository essay for language arts, the students take notes from videos as well as from books and other print resources. In class, they take all their acquired information and write an essay that answers the original question: What would have made the outcome of the Titanic disaster different?[19]

Information Literacy in the Workforce

How do future job projections relate to information literacy? What are the specific implications of information literacy to the workforce? How do business and government leaders compare with leaders in education or business leaders in other countries with regard to their understanding of information literacy?

All projections of future job needs point to the need for more "knowledge workers." It has been estimated that "20 percent of all jobs by the year 2000 will be unfilled unless many of today's workers are retrained to be knowledge workers...whose main value to their employers is to gather, analyze, and disseminate information in such knowledgebased industries such as computers, medical care, communications and instrumentation."[20]

Others argue that all industries and government work will become more intensively knowledge based (i.e., that the more highly global competitive marketplace is the logical outgrowth of the information explosion and the revolution in technology). In keeping with this thinking, the 1991 report of the U.S. Department of Labor's Secretary's Commission on Achieving Necessary Skills, *What Work Requires of Schools: SCANS Report for American 2000*, included the following competencies relating to information:

- *Acquires and Evaluates Information.* Identifies need for data, obtains it from existing sources or creates it, and evaluates its relevance and accuracy.

- *Organizes and Maintains Information.* Organizes, processes, and maintains written or computerized records and other forms of information in a systematic fashion.

- *Interprets and Communicates Information.* Selects and analyzes information and communicates the results to others using oral, written, graphic, pictorial, or multimedia methods.

- *Uses Computers to Process Information.* Employs computers to acquire, organize, analyze, and communicate information.[21]

Building on the competency framework established by the SCANS Report, the U.S. Department of Labor has been supporting the Occupational Information Network (O*NET), an electronic database of occupational information that provides a common language and framework that can be accessed directly by the public as well as employers and educators. The heading of cross-functional skills—defined as those that facilitate performance of activities that occur across all job areas—lists the following skills:

- problem identification;

- information gathering;

- information organization;

- synthesis/reorganization;

- idea generation;

- idea evaluation;

- implementation planning; and

- solution appraisal.[22]

Moreover, because all company and government assets (including technology) except one are commodities—which are equally available to all competitors—the single most valuable resource an organization has is its knowledge workers.[23] People trained to be knowledge workers may fail, however, to identify the right solution or best approach to a situation because they don't have access to the facts they need to make an intelligent decision. In publications ranging from the *Wall Street Journal* to the *Harvard Business Review*, internationally recognized management consultant Peter Drucker continues to warn:

> Executives have become computer-literate. The younger ones, especially, know more about the way the computer works than they know about the mechanics of the automobile or the telephone. But not many executives are information literate. They know how to get data, but most still have to learn how to use data....Few executives yet know how to ask: "What information do I need to do my job? When do I need it? In what form? And from whom should I be getting it?" Fewer still ask: "What new tasks can I tackle now that I have all this data? Which old tasks should I abandon? Which tasks should I do differently?" ...A "database," no matter how copious, is not information. It is information's ore. For raw material to become information, it must be organized for a task, directed toward specific performance, applied to a decision. Raw material cannot do that itself.[24]

Indeed, it would appear from a 1992 study, "Information Management and Japanese Success," that most Japanese business people are more information literate than their American counterparts:

> Information plays a very substantial role in Japan's businesses, as well as in day-to-day life. The Japanese produce and consume books at a world-leading pace, and Japanese companies and government agencies furiously collect information on every conceivable aspect of their environment. (It has been suggested that the Mitsui Corporation's Knowledge Industry Division, the group responsible for business intelligence, is actually superior to the CIA in collecting information.) As a recent commentator has written: "For the Japanese, the statement that knowledge is power is not just a pious truism, it is a basic operating principle."[25]

What information, in fact, do businesses in America generally use for decision making? A scan of the literature on management and information management systems makes clear that many companies place almost exclusive attention on managing internal information. Drucker likens this heavy reliance on internal information to flying on one wing. He points out that "for most CEOs, the most important information is not about customers but about noncustomers."[26] Drucker conceives of executives as having a series of information management tools, among which they must choose to do particular pieces of information generation. For strategy, he says,

> We need organized information about the environment. Strategy has to be based on information about markets, customers, and noncustomers; about technology in one's own industry and others; about worldwide finance; and about the changing world economy. For that is where the results are. Not all of the needed information about the outside is available. But even where information is readily available, many businesses are oblivious to it....
>
> Even big companies, in large part, will have to hire outsiders to help them. To think through what the business needs requires somebody who knows and understands the highly specialized information field. There is far too much information for any but specialists to find their way around. The sources are totally diverse. But most of what enterprises need to know about the environment is obtainable only from outside sources—from all kinds of data banks and data services, from journals in many languages, from trade associations, from government publications, from World Bank reports and scientific papers, and from specialized studies.[27]

What external sources of information are used by most businesses? Do they include the broad array of resources listed by Drucker? No: Research shows that for most small and medium-sized companies, external information comes from people already known to the manager; in fact, "family and friends were judged more valuable sources of information than bankers, lawyers, and accountants." Although managers do consult some impersonal sources of information—the most popular of which are magazines and journals—they rate informal personal information more valuable than formal (expert) or impersonal information.[28] Given this lack of sophistication about information accessing and management, is it any wonder that so many small businesses flounder?

A closer look at information use in the health care sector may better underscore the importance of understanding the need for and actually obtaining external impersonal information to address the issue (or, in this case, the patient) at hand. In a study of physicians, 95 percent of the 28 who returned questionnaires said that the information provided by the hospital contributed to better-informed clinical decisions. More specifically, the following changes in patient care were reported:

	Reported by
Change in advice given to patient	72%
Choice of tests	51%
Choice of drugs	45%
Diagnosis	29%
Reduced length of hospital stay	19%

This finding is a key aspect of the impact study—the use of information to change decisions made. The areas of change ranged from diagnosis to advice given to patients. The latter shows the highest degree of change. Physicians also said that the external information contributed to their ability to avoid the following negative events:

	Reported by
Additional tests or procedures	49%
Additional outpatient visits	26%
Surgery	21%
Patient mortality	19%
Hospital admission	12%

With regard to the health of themselves or their loved ones, information literacy abilities can empower people to ask the right questions of health care providers and to seek additional information if they are not satisfied with the answers they are receiving.

Only recently has the importance of the health care consumer been appreciated. The consumer shares an equal role, along with the provider, as a critical decision maker who drives the entire health care enterprise. We have entered into an era of health care informatics that empowers consumer decision making through the use of emerging interactive and multimedia technologies. These technologies can be distributed to virtually anyone, anywhere, at any time. This new focus is the result of a paradigm change in the delivery of health care. Consumers want to actively participate and partner with health care providers and become an integral part of the decision-making process.[29]

Business Education

Given the highly competitive global economy for which schools of businesses are preparing students, we might expect that they would be campus models for integrating information literacy into their curriculums. An article in the Spring 1996 *Sloan Management Review*, however, questions whether schools of business will ignore changes in the workplace brought on by the Information Age:

> The international data highway will transform business education, although not necessarily its traditional supplier, the business school. Will the business school remain insulated from the knowledge revolution? Will it play a leadership role? Will it wither away?[30]

A summary of the lack of information literacy efforts within schools of business accredited by the American Association of Collegiate Schools of Business is well documented in the September/October 1994 issue of the *Journal of Education for Business* by Douglass K. Hawes (then a faculty member at the University of Wyoming). He reports that the literature review of what is being done in business schools provides a few good practicing models of how information literacy efforts have been integrated into the curriculum—including stand-alone courses—inclusion in capstone courses, and required self-teaching exercises. Nevertheless, Hawes concludes that "today's business school graduate is not being adequately prepared to function in an information literate fashion in a world of knowledge workers."[31]

In a classic chicken-and-egg situation, the question remains, Where will the impetus for preparing effective knowledge workers come from: schools of business or business leadership? At the moment, neither seems to be undergoing significant change—much less assuming a leadership role for the transition—and Peter Drucker remains an unanswered voice in the wilderness suggesting that a knowledge society requires information literate executives who have learned how to learn.

Perhaps the missing leadership will come from a national group of CEOs brought together by the 1998 Aspen Institute Forum on Communications and Society.

Notes

1. Alvin Toffler, *Future Shock* (New York: Bantam, 1970).

2. R. S. Wurman, *Information Anxiety* (New York: Doubleday, 1989).

3. H. E. Meyer, *Real World Intelligence: Organized Information for Executives* (New York: Weidenfield & Nicholson, 1987), p. 24.

4. United States Government, *Budget of the United States Government*, Fiscal Year 1998, available at <www.access.gpo.gov/su_docs/budget/index.html>.

5. W. H. Donald (ed.), *Standard and Poors' Industry Surveys–Publishing, 165*, (New York: S&P Corporation. Oct. 2, 1997), p. 10.

6. UNESCO, *Annuaire Statistique*, 1996, (Paris: UNESCO,1996), p. 6.2.

7. Bureau of the Census, *Statistical Abstracts of the United States*, 1997 (Washington D.C.: U.S. Department of Commerce, 1997), p. 574.

8. T. Davenport and L. Prusak, "Blow Up the Corporate Library," *International Journal of Information Management*, vol. 13, 1993, p. 405.

9. "Business Statistics," *Electronic Business Today* (vol. 23, 1997), p. 20.

10. *Managing End-user Computing: Multi-client Research Study,* (Boston, Mass: Nolan, Norton & Co., 1992), p. 1.

11. T. M. Ciolek, "The Scholarly Uses of the Internet: An Online Survey." (1998), available at <http://coombs.anu.edu/Depts/RSPAS/DIR/PAPERS/Internet-Survey-98.html>.

12. Ibid. p. 21.

13. Association of College and Research Libraries, *A Progress Report on Information Literacy: Final Report*, (Chicago, IL: American Library Association, 1998).

14. American Library Association, *ALA Presidential Committee on Information Literacy: Final Report*, (Chicago, IL.: American Library Association, 1989), p. 7.

15. K. Fulton, *Learning in the Digital Age: Insights Into the Issues*. (Santa Monica, Calif.: Milken Family Foundation, 1997), available: <http://www.milkenexchange.org>.

16. N. Mueller, "Missing the Competitive-advantage Boat," *Managing Office Technology*, vol. 42, (1997), p. 33.

17. P. S. Breivik, *Student Learning in an Information Age*, (Phoenix: Oryx, 1998), pp. 16, 17.

18. T. Wesley, "Teaching Library Research: Are We Preparing Students for Effective Information Use?" *Emergency Librarian*, vol. 18, 1991, pp. 29-30.

19. P. S. Breivik and J. A. Senn, *Information Literacy: Educating Children for the 21st Century*, (New York: Scholastic, 1994), p. 29.

20. Christian & Timbers, Inc., "Knowledge Workers in Demand Through the Year 2000," *Managing Office Technology*, vol. 42, (1997), p. 22.

21. U.S. Department of Labor, Secretary's Commission on Achieving Necessary Skills, *What Work Requires of Schools: A SCANS Report for America 2000*, (Washington, D.C.: U.S. General Printing Office), 1991.

22. U.S. Department of Labor, Occupational Information Network (1998), available at <http://www.doleta.gov/programs/ONET>.

23. A. M. Webber, "What's So New About the New Economy?" *Harvard Business Review*, vol. 71, (1993), pp. 24-32.

24. P. Drucker, "Be Data Literate—Know What To Know," *Wall Street Journal*, December 12, 1992, 16:3.

25. L. Prusak and J. Matarazzo, *Information Management and Japanese Success*, (Washington, D.C.. Special Libraries Association, 1992), p. 1.

26. P. Drucker, "Infoliteracy," *Forbes*, vol. 154, 1994, p. 109.

27. P. Drucker, "The Information Executives Truly Need," *Harvard Business Review*, vol. 73, (1994), p. 61.

28. L. Smeltzer, "Environmental Scanning Practices in Small Business," *Journal of Small Business Management*, July 1988, pp. 55-63.

29. P. S. Breivik, *Student Learning in the Information Age*, (Phoenix: Oryx, 1998), p. 68.

30. B. Ives and L. Jarvenpaa, "Will the Internet Revolutionize Business Education and Research?" *Sloan Management Review*, vol. 37, 1996, pp. 33-41.

31. D. Hawes, "Information Literacy and the Business Schools," *Journal of Education for Business*, vol. 6, 1994, p. 138.

Forum on Communications and Society
1998 Annual Meeting

Conference Participants
August 7-9, 1998
Aspen, Colorado

C. Michael Armstrong
Chairman and CEO
AT&T

Zoë Baird
President
The John and Mary R. Markle
  Foundation

James Barr III
President and CEO
TDS TELECOM

Asa Briggs
Former Chancellor
British Open University
  and
Member
British House of Lords

David V. B. Britt
President and CEO
Children's Television
  Workshop

Jolynn Barry Butler
President
National Association of
  Regulatory Utility
  Commissioners

John Doerr
Partner
Kleiner Perkins Caufield
  & Byers

Ira Fishman
Chief Executive Officer
Schools and Libraries
  Corporation

Stanley Hubbard
Chairman, President, and CEO
Hubbard Broadcasting

Reed E. Hundt
FOCAS Co-Chair
Principal
Charles Ross Partners, LLC

Michael H. Jordan
Chairman and CEO
CBS Corporation

William Kennard
Chairman
Federal Communications
  Commission

Charles B. Knapp
President
The Aspen Institute

Michael O. Leavitt
Governor
State of Utah

Edward J. Markey
Member
United States House of
    Representatives

William Milliken
President
Communities In Schools

Peter Price
President
Television USA

Rebecca Rimel
President and CEO
The Pew Charitable Trusts

Eric Schmidt
FOCAS Co-Chair
Chairman and CEO
Novell, Inc.

Kurt Schmoke
Mayor
City of Baltimore, Maryland

Mark Warner
Managing Director
Columbia Capital Corporation

Lois Jean White
President
The National PTA

Resource Participant:

Martin L. Ernst
Research Affiliate
Program on Information
    Resources Policy
Harvard University

Moderator:

Charles M. Firestone
Executive Vice President
Policy Programs
    and
Executive Director
Communications and Society
    Program
The Aspen Institute

Rapporteur:

Richard Adler
President
People and Technology

Staff:

Amy Garmer
Associate Director
Communications and Society
    Program
The Aspen Institute

Elizabeth Golder
Senior Program Coordinator
Communications and Society
    Program
The Aspen Institute

Note: Titles and affiliations are as of date of conference.

Acknowledgments

Prior to the annual meeting, each FOCAS member selects one representative from his or her organization to attend a two-day planning session with experts to prepare for the annual conference. This preparatory session provides the FOCAS annual meeting with a considered agenda and a succinct background report. We are grateful to the individuals listed below, who attended the preparatory session in April 1998 and whose knowledge and expertise were instrumental in shaping the 1998 conference agenda and, ultimately, this report.

Forum on Communications and Society
Preparatory Session • April 16-18, 1998
Queenstown, Maryland

List of Participants

Peter Bankson
Vice President
Information Technology
Communities In Schools

Patricia Senn Breivik
Dean
University Libraries
Wayne State University

John Buffalo
Senior Manager
Corporate Communications
Discovery Channel

Harold C. Crump
Vice President
Corporate Affairs
Hubbard Broadcasting, Inc.

Michael Eisenberg
Director
ERIC Clearinghouse on
    Information and Technology

Charles M. Firestone
Director
Communications and Society
    Program
The Aspen Institute

Maggi Gaines
Executive Director
Baltimore Reads, Inc.

Amy Korzick Garmer
Assistant Director
Communications and Society
    Program
The Aspen Institute

Renée Hobbs
Associate Professor
Babson College

Doris McCarter
Telecommunications Specialist
Telecommunications Division
Public Utilities Commission
    of Ohio

Virginia Gehr McEnerney
Director
Community Relations
Time Warner Inc.

Bernadette McGuire-Rivera
Associate Administrator
National Telecommunications
    and Information
    Administration
U.S. Department of Commerce

David Morse
Director
Public Affairs
The Pew Charitable Trusts

John Orlando
Vice President, Washington
CBS Corporation

Nancy Pelz-Paget
Director
Program on Education in a
    Changing Society
The Aspen Institute

Andrew S. Petersen
Manager, Federal Relations
TDS Telecommunications
    Corporation

Marilyn Reznick
Vice President, Education
AT&T Foundation

Arthur Sheekey
Acting Director
Learning Technologies on
    Telecommunications
Council of Chief State
    Schools Officers

Timothy R. Walter
Project Director
Rural Economic Policy
    Program
The Aspen Institute

Staff:

Elizabeth Golder
Program Coordinator
Communications and Society
    Program
The Aspen Institute

Note: Titles and affiliations are as of date of conference.

About the Authors

Richard Adler is president of People & Technology, a media research and consulting firm in Palo Alto, California. He also serves as Futurist-in-Residence for the InfoWorld Futures Project (www.infoworld.com). In addition, he has held senior positions at SeniorNet, the Institute for the Future, and The Aspen Institute Communications and Society Program. In addition, he has taught at Stanford, University of California at Los Angeles, and Oberlin College.

Adler has written extensively on the subject of new information technologies. His publication credits include *Jobs, Technology, and Employability: Redefining the Social Contract* (The Aspen Institute, 1998), *The Future of Advertising: New Approaches to the Attention Economy* (The Aspen Institute, 1998), "Wonderful Internet Life" (introduction to the *1997-98 Interactive Sourcebook*, North America Publishing, 1997), *Older Americans and Computers* (SeniorNet, 1996), and *Opportunities in Videotex: A Guide to Communicating and Marketing Through Electronic Services* (ISA, 1989).

He holds a B.A. degree from Harvard University, an M.A. degree from the University of California at Berkeley, and an M.B.A. degree from the McLaren School of Business at the University of San Francisco.

Patricia Senn Breivik serves as dean of the University Libraries at Wayne State University and as chief administrative officer in charge of five University libraries, Media Services, the University Press, the Library Information Science Program and the Office for Teaching and Learning. Her previous positions include associate vice president for Information Resources at the Towson State University, director of library and telecommunications services supporting the Auraria campus in Denver, and as part-time special assistant to the president of the University of Colorado.

Currently, Breivik serves as chair of the National Forum on Information Literacy. She is past President of the Association of College and Research Libraries. A frequent speaker and writer on the topic of information literacy and resource-based learning, she is co-author of *Information Literacy Revolution in the Library* and author of *Student Learning in the Information Age*. Breivik holds a B.A. degree from Brooklyn College, an M.L.S. degree from Pratt Institute, and a D.L.S. degree from Columbia University.

The Aspen Institute
Communications and Society Program

The overall goal of the Communications and Society Program is to promote thoughtful, values-based decision making in the fields of communications, media, and information policy. In particular, the Program focuses on the implications of communications and information technologies on democratic institutions, individual behavior, instruments of commerce, and community life.

The Communications and Society Program accomplishes this goal through two main types of activities. First, it brings together leaders of industry, government, the nonprofit sector, media organizations, the academic world, and others for roundtable meetings to assess the impact of modern communications and information systems on the ideas and practices of a democratic society. Second, the Program promotes research and distributes conference reports to decision makers in the communications and information fields, both within the United States and internationally, and to the public at large.

Topics addressed by the Program vary as issues and the policy environment evolve, but each project seeks to achieve a better understanding of the societal impact of the communications and information infrastructures, to foster a more informed and participatory environment for communications policymaking, or to promote the use of communications for global understanding. In recent years, the Communications and Society Program has chosen to focus with special interest on the issues of electronic democracy, lifelong learning and technology, electronic commerce, Internet policy, and the role of the media in democratic society.

The Program also coordinates all of the activities of the Institute for Information Studies, a joint program with Nortel Networks, and engages in other domestic and international initiatives related to communications and information technology and policy.